The "**L**ogic" of **H**appiness

To our Good Friends, Rodger & Sue

May you always be filled with Love, Peace, Joy & the Spirit.

Your Friends always-

Joseph & Linda

The "Logic" of Happiness

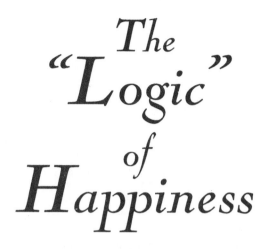

PROVERBS *and*
PRACTICAL
WISDOM
for SPIRITUAL
LIVING

PHILIP ST. ROMAIN

TRIUMPH™ BOOKS
Liguori, Missouri

Published by Triumph™ Books
Liguori, Missouri
An Imprint of Liguori Publications

Library of Congress Cataloging-in-Publication Data

St. Romain, Philip A.
    The logic of happiness : proverbs and practical wisdom for
spiritual living / by Philip St. Romain.
        p.   cm.
    ISBN 0-89243-687-5
    1. Meditations.   2. Spiritual life—Christianity—Quotations,
maxims, etc.   I. Title.
BV4832.2.S747   1994
242—dc20   94-7493
                                                              CIP

Printed in the United States of America

First Edition

Contents

Part I
Meditations on the Mystery of Faith and Existence

Contents

Part II
Dynamics of Mystical Transformation

Part III
Exercises for Breaking Free

Part IV
Nuggets from the Stream of Life

Foreword

My "logic" of happiness can best be summarized as follows:

- 🍂 If you're going to be alive anyway, why be miserable? Why not be as happy as possible every moment of the day?

- 🍂 If there is heaven, then your happiness goes on and on. If not, then is it not still better to pass the time in joy than in sadness?

- 🍂 If you would be happy, then you must also learn about what happiness is, and what stops you from being happy.

- 🍂 What stops you from being happy is the belief that you lack something necessary for happiness. You have placed a condition on happiness, and you perceive that condition to be lacking.

- 🍂 Unhappiness is conditioned, judgmental, rejecting of the NOW, self-focused.

🖋 If unhappiness is so, then happiness cannot exist unless this situation is reversed. Happiness must be something that is unconditioned, nonjudgmental, accepting of the NOW, loving.

🖋 Only God is unconditioned, nonjudgmental, NOW, loving.

🖋 To be happy is to be like God.

🖋 To be like God, you must be with-God.

🖋 To be with-God, you must be where God is, when God is there, as God is there.

🖋 Since God is always-here/now/as-love, to be happy, you must be-here/now/in-love.

🖋 God is here.
God is NOW.
God is loving everyone and everything without judgment or reserve.

🖋 Where are you?

🖋 What are you doing?

🖋 What are you waiting for?

This meditation, as indeed the message of this book, is a message that has been impressed on me most forcefully through my own lived experience as a Christian contemplative who also happens to be a married layman and the father of three children. Marriage, fatherhood, and working in the world have kept my feet on the ground, while contemplative spirituality has opened my mind to receive occasional glimpses of the truth. These intuitions, which come from years of contemplation and journaling, are the source of this collection of proverbs and meditations.

Christianity is both practical and mystical. How could it be otherwise? Truth is one! Truth that is mystical ought not be impractical, and truth that is practical ought not lead away from mystical contemplation. The Second Person of the Trinity — a most mystical character by any standards — came to know the ways of carpentry in the person of Jesus. It is only a false or non-Christian mysticism that is impractical in the sense of fostering imprudent and anti-worldly attitudes. The God of Christianity is to be found here, now, lovingly involved in all of the affairs of creation.

The contemplative journey takes us deep into the soul, where the mystery of the self and the mystery of God are so intertwined as to seem one life. My primary reason for publishing these meditations is to share what I have learned in my explorations of these depths. I am convinced that every person may come to know and experience enlightenment and contemplation, the two great mystical experiences of East and West. These writings probe the similarities and differences between these two experiences. They are intended to invite the reader to "come and see" the truth behind the words. Conceptual understanding is not enough. But words can serve as a springboard off of which we may leap into realms of mystery that words can never capture.

That is what I hope for you, the reader: that these words will help to form in you a contemplative attitude open to the mystery of loving Silence. If a particular proverb, passage, or meditation does not seem helpful to you at this time, leave it alone and find one that does. Also, do not accept anything in this book as true without testing it for yourself. Secondhand truth is worthless! We are persons, not parrots! Truth must be known in your own heart if it is to grow in you.

May you be grown! And may God use these words to help you to grow.

Part I

Meditations on the Mystery
of Faith and Existence

Cling to nothing. Consciousness unfolds in stages and in ways you cannot even predict. There are times for thinking, times for studying, times for being sensately present, times for creativity, times for feeling, times for being lost in emptiness. It is all important. Let it happen as it will. Follow your heart. Don't force anything.

The Growth Process

From beginning to end, the process of growth lies outside the range of our capacity to exercise absolute control. From the production of gametes, to the fertilization of the egg, to the division of the zygote, to cellular differentiation, to organic homeostasis, through Erikson's, Loevinger's, Kohlberg's, Maslow's, and Piaget's stages of growth, to recovery from sicknesses, to energy upheavals and resolutions, to death and beyond: We do not possess the ability to control these movements of life.

We may affect the growth process — usually for the worse — through the exercise of will: trying to make ourselves into someone, in our own image and likeness. We may also experience our own unfolding and marvel at what is happening.

Therefore, the best course of action is always complete surrender and docility to the growth process. This "way" is not always clear, but it will reveal itself if we are willing to follow the path of love, serenity, and truth. Is this not, in the end, precisely The Way?

If you do not know what to do, then wait for the answer in openness, cherishing the questions in gentleness.

CONSCIOUSNESS AND SPIRITUALITY

Consciousness pertains to states of awareness, and there are many to be experienced along the way. Physiology, diet, and temperament play a big role in determining states of consciousness. So do personal judgments about what is happening to me.

Spirituality pertains to the quality of consciousness, which is directly related to the intent of consciousness. Is consciousness peaceful, open to life, willing to share? Or is it self-focused, closed, irritable, fearful?

Growth in consciousness enables a more mature spirituality. The more awareness and giftedness, the more there is to share.

But growth in consciousness does not guarantee love. Love, however, will eventually produce growth in consciousness.

A consciousness brought forth in love cannot be sustained in nonlove. It will be lost and degenerate into a lower, animal state. It can still be powerful and even evidence psychic gifts. But if there is no love, there is no true human being.

I constrict my consciousness, therefore I am: *the Fall of Humanity!*

An Inventory of Consciousness

The senses are for being-here/now, in loving silence.

The intellect is a talking computer, to store information and solve problems.

The intuitive function is to explore possibilities and to see the truth directly.

Self-image is the product of the intellect, a picture in the computer.

Feelings are the energy context of meaning.

Kundalini is the soul energy, pushing unto growth.

Awareness is the light by means of which you see.

Will is the ability to direct energy this way or that.

High thinking is discriminatory — separate from intellect but connected to it.

"I" am a living soul, the one who "owns" all these functions.

And yet . . . "I" does not create itself. Its "is-ness" is "received" in each moment from the hand of the One who gives life and form.

It is okay to think, feel, desire, remember, or do anything — just so it is not done "in sleep." Enlightenment is not concentration on the now, nor is it only sensate awareness. It is simple awareness. That is all.

DESTINY

You do not know what God has created. You do not possess full knowledge of your potentialities. Therefore, it is best to remain open to your own, continuing unfolding.

Do not limit your possibilities through a narrow projecting of your giftedness and self-image. Instead, follow the lead of your heart.

Allow your destiny to unfold of its own accord. Set no rigid goals about where you "should be" in five years. Simply continue to develop your talents one day at a time "here/now/in-love." The Spirit will lead you to where you are needed and where you may grow. God

knows what God has created, and Go
bring you to fruition.

A baby doesn't have to do anything to be born.
If it "tries" to help out, it only hurts itself.
Trust!

ABOUT GOD

About God, believe only this:

1. That God exists in a realm transcendent to
   what the senses can perceive. This realm
   includes the interiority of the soul.

2. That God creates this world through
   atoms, molecules, cells, and organs, and
   gives consciousness as the creative force
   and guidance within all these levels.

3. That God only loves. The pains of growth
   and injustice do not negate this reality.

4. That Christ is God-incarnate, taking on
   our nature.

5. That evolution now unfolds "in-Christ."
   With Christ, a new evolutionary epoch has
   begun.

6. That Christ and the Father are bonded in the Holy Spirit, whose presence within guides and transforms our own human spirits.

7. That Eucharist is Christ's risen body and the medium through which Christ becomes enfleshed in humans.

8. That, therefore, God is to be trusted, loved, and enjoyed as both dual and nondual Partner.

"Why do I love You? Why do You love me? How can there be two, happy as we?" Just because!

TRUE SPIRITUALITY

To be where God is, as God is, as I am, and to eliminate all that prevents this:

1. Attachment desire — centers attention in the past or the future, where God is not.

2. Interpretive, judgmental conceptualization — violates the simplicity of "as God is." Centers attention in the intellect.

3. Shame, fear, and resentment — give rise to the false self, which is not "as I am."

You are free to learn anything and do anything. There are no conditions for experiencing enlightenment except to eliminate the above. Of course, that's the problem, and the reason why morality and right lifestyle are so important.

Yet the goal should never be forgotten, and the goal is to eventually let go of all attachments . . . to be walking on water.

Leave off everything except that, in this Now-moment, you are totally, enormously loved by God: unity!

KNOWING AND UNKNOWING

You do not need to understand the deep metaphysical question. You cannot, anyway! The best theories are only maps. Real meaning does not come from having the best map.

In the end, all you can say is, "God is. Here I am, too, living. Suffering is unpleasant and to be avoided unless required by integrity. Love is fulfilling. Christ is here to support me. Helping others keeps me out of myopic self-concern.

Working to form a healthy developmental environment for all makes sense." That's really all we know, and this knowledge is more about doing than understanding.

Could it be that true wisdom is practical rather than philosophical?

All real understanding must come from experience if it is not to be distorting of experience. Understanding that comes from conceptualization alone forces reality into compartments and molds created by the mind. This is illusion!

THE CROSS

True spirituality is Love.

The obstacles to spiritual growth are selfishness, preoccupation, anxiety, and various forms of material and psychological idolatry.

When one is centered in love and willing to love, the energies of the false self and its disordered desires confront one daily.

The journey is fun as long as it is easy. When Love calls for one to hang in there, or to do something one does not want to do — even hates to do — then there is a civil war within.

The Cross is the suffering one must endure to

remain true to Love. It is the confrontation of one's own inner hostility and selfishness; it is the confrontation with a sick, sick world.

Through carrying this Cross, one loses the attraction to sin, and becomes transformed — raised up, as it were — in love.

What is this inner resistance to loving without reserve?
   Sin!
   What is its root?
   The fearful false self!
   How to get rid of the false self?
   The Cross: Love that endures even in the face of pain.

EMPTY LOVINGNESS

There is no salvation in physical health, material prosperity, or rational conceptualization. Only in total surrender to God is salvation known.

Only Love is happiness. The higher states of consciousness do not bring happiness except insofar as they express Love.

Therefore, the only way to live is to stand completely naked in this moment, with no crutches or attachments, willing to give and receive life, allowing the Spirit to form you. This nakedness must be whole body-mind-spirit, so that attention is not identified with any level of consciousness but diffused into them all. There must be no self-contraction, no defensiveness, no preconceptions. Breathe deeply, accepting life and returning it holistically.

This is poverty of spirit — to cling to nothing while permitting God's action within. Only when we are in this condition can Love do its mysterious work. Only when we are in this condition can the True Self be realized.

No need for anxiety! All is well in God. The worst that can happen cannot undo this truth.

HAPPINESS AND THE TRUE SELF

In life, there are many problems. The world is unrelenting in its assault. Then there are sickness, death, rain, floods, tornadoes. If any of these are not happening, there is always the risk.

The tragedy is to reserve being okay until there are no problems. Even were such a goal reached, there would be the dynamic of "I'll be okay when..." to contend with, as it focuses now on preventing problems.

No! There is only to accept the inevitable and do what has to be done — here/now/in-love. Living in the True Self is the pearl of great price, and it is not contingent on the absence of problems. Its only conditions are present-moment awareness, an open heart, conceptual open-mindedness, and a willingness to be grown anew by God.

Happiness is unconditioned consciousness. Stop disturbing yourself, and you will be happy.

MY LIFE'S WORK

So far as I can see, there is no other way for me to be happy but to love and serve my family, and to place myself at their disposal for their growth.

That cared for — an enormous task, to be sure — the same goes for my larger family, the Church. I am here to serve with my gifts and talents, to help others to grow.

The same goes for the whole human race and the planet.

I am a vessel through which God's love may

flow. This is my happiness and my work. It is God who has forged me into this vessel, that I might enjoy the sanity and blessedness of giving.

Neither heaven nor enlightenment can be had at the expense of your family. God is living in your family. Where are you living?

SANITY

True sanity comes not from intellectual certainty or self-assurance (which is almost always contrived), but from unrelenting self-honesty in loving acceptance.

Ultimately, you are a mystery, at-one-with-God and so undefinable.

The only true sanity is to be found in honestly accepting what you are experiencing now as you struggle to be lovingly engaged in the reality of the moment. It's okay to remember and plan, but no nostalgia, and no projecting.

God is your sanity. You do not possess sanity. You are sane — even when in pain — when you surrender to the inevitable in love.

Abandon yourself to the care of God. If your brain gets sick or your organ systems make you mentally unstable, that is dis-ease, not insanity. Christ will preserve you and renew you in the end.

There is no such thing as "self-possession." The only self that is stable is the one that emerges in ongoing loving surrender, for this self can never be taken away.

IGNORANT WISDOM

The temptation is to get the conceptual paradigm all defined and then to live out its implications. This is the thorn of the Mental Ego. It once served a purpose, but now it is useless.

Christ calls you to walk in his way. Then will understanding be given.

The truth is that we do not really know conceptually what *is*. We only know from revelation that it is friendly, creative loving — personal.

Conceptualization is a way of organizing information in the service of language. It is also a kind of understanding, and it can point attention in the right direction. Beyond this, however, it is of no use. Once you see the moon, you must quit looking at the finger that points to it and quit reading what the blind say about it. You simply look, and the understanding comes of its own accord.

Can the butterfly be seen in the caterpillar? Not by other caterpillars, it cannot. It can be seen only with butterfly eyes.

MY WAY

The old way was to cultivate an Ideal Self/ Ego focused in Christ through reading, reflection, and dialogue, then to apply the will in the direction of this ideal — or, better, to be drawn by the inner idealization unto its realization, naturally.

This way of focusing, projecting, and walking is no longer my way. I do not know what has happened to that old ideal Self. Perhaps it is still there as an infrastructure, holding things together in some manner.

The new way of walking is less structured. It is to be here/now/in-love, to drop all that prevents this, and to respond from the level of the flesh to the needs presenting in each moment. Thinking and problem solving have their place, but it seems that intuition runs the show. Too much thinking clouds intuition.

Dare I trust my intuition? As long as I do not do what I know to be wrong, then why not? No other approach to life brings serenity and happiness now.

After a while, there is nothing to be learned in reflective thinking. Only deep, intuitive listening and trust in your inner wisdom will yield the truth as you need to know it at this time.

SPIRITUAL EVOLUTION

It is God who grows us through the dynamic of needs and their fulfillment. Dependent creatures, we experience our neediness for a wide number of things. The manner in which we meet these needs determines what kind of people we become. Our needs change as we grow, and so we continue pursuing them, changing and evolving as we do so.

There is a general tendency to need less if the journey proceeds along moral lines. Simplicity is the mark of a saint. Fresh water, wholesome food, a roof, a fire, a few friends, Eucharist, times for silence, meaningful work — these are of the essence, and there is no disposing of them without seriously impairing the quality of life.

Meet your needs in a healthy, loving manner, and help others to do so as well. Feel your needs, and don't try to force your growth in any direction. Simply live well, and your growth will unfold of its own accord.

Every person is a Self-becoming. If you know this for yourself, you will see it in others.

CONTROL

You control nothing!

Nothing!

You could die tonight.

You could get a brain disease and go insane.

Your wife and/or children could die, get very sick, or become very disturbed.

The economy could fail, leaving you destitute.

The nations could war and destroy the environment that supports you.

You could be fired from your job, or find yourself working for an incompetent boss.

You can prevent none of these from happening. If they do not happen, it is grace, or luck, and you should be grateful.

The only control you have is in your willingness to be here now in love. Sick or healthy, this you can do. All the rest is circumstantial, contingent, and unpredictable.

Do not, for one second, ever trust in your virtuousness and humility. Trust only in Christ's ability to keep you straight.

SINGLE SEEING

Looking out at the world through these eyes. The eyes are like windows.

Who peers through them?

An old, familiar soul.

An infant, waking up.

Me! Just-me! That is all.

And what I see, I see without illusion — fresh, clean, here, now.

There is no interpretation, no judgment, no projection, no conceptual filtering.

There is just-me, and whatever I am looking at, and this is the universe.

It is beautiful! That which God has created is

very, very good. The one who sees is good; that which is seen is good; the seeing is good.

The brain becomes clear, the heart warm, the gut relaxed. There is nothing to fear. This moment is all there is. It is Eternal Life.

Just look! Don't analyze. There is nothing to know. See with your eyes, not your intellect. Let things be. This is the way to experience the simplicity of existence.

THE SOUL SELF

The soul is the source of mind and body. It is also expressed as mind and body. Body and mind are contained in the soul.

The essence of the soul is awareness and freedom. These are spiritual qualities that can be experienced directly in deep silence. Most of us, however, experience them indirectly by means of the operations of the spirit through mind and body.

The direct experience of the soul self is "That I am." This is qualitatively different from the experience of "Who I am," which is the ego self. The knowledge "That I am" allows one great inner freedom and a sense of the unity of all things. It also awakens in one a sense "That God is," for my "That-ness" is received in each moment from God. This sense of God, however, becomes more explicit and personal through faith and prayer.

To know "That I am" is to know immortality. "That-ness" is not a consequence of the flesh, which will pass away. "That I am" does not come and go. It always "Is."

The "I" who sees cannot be defined, but it can be experienced. Enjoy it, and there "you" are.

HOPE FOR A SICK SOUL

A diseased body can be easily defined in terms of failure in organ systems and tissues.

A diseased mind is weak, confused, undisciplined, attached to many things, a volcano of negative thoughts and emotions.

A sick spirit is hopeless.

The body and mind cannot heal when the spirit is hopeless. Any "cure" will be short-lived.

A sick body and mind can lead to a sick spirit. A sick mind can produce a sick body.

How to dispel hopelessness?

Through belief in life's meaning.

Why believe in life's meaning when evil, suffering, and death exist?

Because Christ is risen.

How do we know this?

Believe, and you will see.

Do you believe God's will is your happiness? If not, then whose will is?

NOWHERE TO GO

There is nowhere to go and nothing to do to be happy. There is only to do "whatever," pleasant or unpleasant, in union with God. Practically speaking, this means to do what I am doing and nothing else — to do it with an open heart and nonjudgmental mind.

The purpose of prayer, then, is to become entrained in this manner of living. In prayer, all preconceptions, good ideas, and projections are encountered in the silence. I see them and let them go. To simply breathe in God's love, open in all levels of being, letting God form me, submitting any self-movement to the Spirit — that is entrainment for happiness.

34

God cannot be experienced through your efforts, meditations, and ascetical techniques. The most you can do is come to receptive silence. Whatever God reveals is up to God.

TRUE PRAYER

In all my prayers, I shall remember:

1. That I am a creature, a contingent being, entirely dependent on God for my existence.

2. That my own ascetical practices apart from love of God only make me more self-righteous and less open to intimacy.

3. That God is an undefinable Mystery.

4. That my intent in prayer needs to be affirming of God as Creator, and inviting the Spirit to work in my soul to make me a Christ. A short, simple "Yes, Lord," spoken not with the lips but in the silence of the heart, may summarize all of the above.

The stream knows where it is going, and the raft of Christ will hold. Stay on board. Trust! Have fun!

A PRAYER FOR UNITY

O Lord, my God.
You want to see in me?
You want me to participate in your seeing?
You want to love in me?
You want me to participate in your loving?
You want to "be" in me?
You want me to participate in your being?
You need my yes for this?
I say yes, my Lord.
See, love, and be in me.
Enable me to see with your seeing,
   to love with your loving,
   to be with your being,
that you may extend your reign through me,
and I may know the glory
you would share with me.

Con-templa-tion is joining templates — Christ's loving openness with my own attention. Rest in him and be healed.

"I Am"

This is the affirmation of the fact of my existence as a person. It is also God's affirmation of existence as a person.

Only a person can say and know the meaning of "I am."

To attempt to define or explain "I am" is to reduce it and annihilate the mystery. Do not say, "I am a husband," or "I am a writer." Rather, say, "I husband," or "I write."

Personhood is not something you do, neither is it here or there. It is who you are, and it is in every cell of your body.

Be a person. Rest in the mystery, "That I am."

No self-definition, no ego. Allow God to define you, and you will know yourself.

The Self

"I" am a light shining brightly
   a here/now presence
   indivisible into parts
   an energy animating a body
   a body emanating spiritual energy

a living intelligence
a freedom amid conditioning
the one who sees through these eyes.
And God: Where is God?
God is in the self.
The self is in God.
And yet, the self is not-God:
It knows not the secrets of the universe;
it creates not its own existence;
it has not power beyond its own freedom
and knowledge;
it exists only in a limited sphere.
God and I are not-one, not-two.
"God is"; "I am"; "We are."

The eyes are windows. Who is peering out of
them? Experience this, but do not try to define it.

ENLIGHTENMENT

This is the natural, awakened state of a person. It happens of its own accord when one lives unintentionally in the NOW.

Nonintentional living happens when the disturbance of judgmental thinking is dropped.

Judgmental thinking is dropped when the past is healed through forgiveness and, after prudent planning, the future is left to itself. One must also make many decisions to drop unnecessary thinking, and to never indulge judging as good or bad that which is neither good nor bad — except in reference to the ego.

All this may be done outside of the context of formal religious practices. Formal religious practices might even serve to negate this liberation.

Enlightenment is not love, nor is it mystical contemplation, for these are experienced in relationship. But enlightenment is the perfect context for relationship since self-centered projections and demands are out of the way. Love flowers most beautifully in the good soils of an enlightened soul!

Be ye enlightened, O Christian brothers and sisters! Accept the gift of the East. Be-here/now, and love will be born.

Just be here now, in the body, from the heart, without needing to "get" anything, and you will know the True Self.

SELF AND NO-SELF

Enlightenment is the loss of the experience of the reflective, intentional self. There is no longer a sense of a solid or boundaried self, and yet there is the other, who is "not-me." There are also all these actions I do, for which I must take responsibility.

And so the intellect affirms that even in enlightenment, there is an individual agent of choice who is not the other. Neither is this choosing a robotic spinning out of conditioning. Were that the case, one would be less free in enlightenment than before.

If robotic conditioning is not doing the choosing, and the reflective, intentional ego is not doing the choosing, then who is making the choices I make all day long, and what is the process by means of which such choices are made?

It seems as though the right action emerges spontaneously in response to the needs of the moment.

Who responds?

Hush now, or you'll fall asleep.

Never, ever stop believing that you are! If you are not, then who is there to accept responsibility for your behavior?

God?
Absurd!
The conditioned mind?
Whose conditioned mind?
Yours!

CHRISTIAN ENLIGHTENMENT

"Do as he tells you," Our Lady said.

Live the Great Sermon, and enlightenment will come in due time.

The specific contributions Jesus makes unto this end:

- His constant supportive friendship

- His Spirit within to renew and configure the soul in his own image

- His Flesh and Blood, to graft us into his Mystical Body and order our energies accordingly

- His own knowledge of the Creator as Personal, Loving Being

🍂 His Church — other people with whom to journey and celebrate

🍂 Sound teaching to strengthen and properly orient the mind

We have, here, a Master through whom the whole universe will be renewed. Only he can bear the full vision and live as human flesh.

Who among the Eastern masters can equal Christ?

Entrust your soul to him, and to him alone. The rest can only give you what they know, which is in no way superior to his enlightenment.

> To be or to love? East or West?
> To be-in-love. This is best.

SELF AND GOD

The objective pole of self is self-image/concept, ego.

The subjective pole cannot be seen, for it is the see-er. Nevertheless, its characteristics are freedom, mystery, and personality, meaning here a capacity to love.

The objective self is awake to particularity. The subjective self is awake at the level of existence, oneness. The energetic bond between the two is libido, or psychic energy.

God's subjectivity is the Father. God's objectification is the universe and, especially, the Son, who is the Image of the unseen (but seeing) God. Christ is God's Self-Image, as it were. Through him, we come to that mysterious Subjectivity who is the Person Jesus called Father. The energy bond between Father and Son is the Spirit, who testifies to both.

Jesus knew all of the above. In him, human and divine subjectivity and objectivity were one. To see him is to see the divine image in human form. To behold his gaze is to see the personal quality of his human/divine soul. To grow close to him is to become like him...to know what he knows as he knows.

Your being is an "eye" through which God sees creation. God wants to know creation in and through you. In doing so, you come to see with God's seeing, know with God's knowing, love with God's loving. This is the meaning of incarnational spirituality.

43

RELATIONALITY

God is Trinity. Hence, a human being, who is a God-imager, is also essentially relational.

This means that the fullest development of mystical enlightenment can be realized only in community, and not in simple awareness. The nonjudgmental attitude of enlightenment is fertile ground for relationships but often unmoved to engage itself so. Being-in-potency must give rise to being-in-action or else it becomes rancid. It is not enough to be-here-now; you must also be-in-love.

We are made for love. We must drop our attachments — yes — but then we must see the other, dialogue, negotiate, feel, lend a helping hand. We do this not out of a superegoic sense of duty, or, less, to make ourselves worthy of being loved. We engage in the struggle to build community because *this* is the completion of the enlightenment experience and the fulfillment of all our desires for happiness. In the engagement to build community, the personal quality of the True Self is awakened and the personal quality of God's love realized. All of the faculties of the soul become molded together in one working whole, whose root is love. No one faculty is to be preferred, none neglected. Love itself will order them now.

Spiritual disciplines that produce the fruit of relationship avoidance are to be trashed, even if they lead to states of sublime awareness and contentment.

"I" TO "I"

For me, the human "I" is the observer-in-freedom; the "I" sees (awareness) and chooses the direction of its seeing (freedom). A state of consciousness, then, can be viewed as an energetic medium in which the "I" experiences and exercises itself. The "I" sees and moves in and out of psychosomatic states; it transcends them while being immanent within them. For the unenlightened, states of consciousness might be considered experiences of the "I," but this is delusion and attachment of "I-to-states." "I" is "that" which moves in and out of states of consciousness.

The direct, nonconceptual, unmediated experience of the "I" is what Zen calls enlightenment. It is a spiritual experience because the "I" is a direct creation of God; it cannot be derived from other states. The "I" simply "is"; it does not create itself but "receives" its existence in each moment. From whence or whom comes its existence? The Buddhist is silent on this point, encouraging us to enjoy the wonder of the seeing "I."

In Christian faith, the "I" realizes that it, too, is seen and chosen by another "I," the Father who sees all, including the "I," whom the Father has created through his Logos, or Christ. Of course, it goes without saying that most Christian mystics experience their faith in an unenlightened state, their "I" strongly attached to a Christian self-image. That's what most Buddhists see of Christians, and so they rightly recognize that most Christian mystics are still operating in some degree of illusion concerning the experience of "I." The enlightened Buddhist knows the "I" directly, and knows this as the most mysterious of human experiences. The unenlightened Christian mystic knows something of the wonder of God through faith and believes this to be the most beautiful of experiences. And so, in most cases, both Buddhist and Christian have accused the other of having the short end of the stick. This is most unfortunate, for each is talking about a different experience.

Since Buddhism and Christian mysticism describe different experiences, one must ask if these experiences are opposed to each other. The answer here is clearly no, for the "I" that the Christian knows indirectly as the object of God's love is none other than the very same "I" that the Buddhist knows as the subject of attention. Christian enlightenment, then, is both experiences happening simultaneously and harmoniously — the enlightened "I" knowing itself as the "beloved" of God. It is the experience of the mystical, transcendent "Thou" of God by an awakened "I." Christian enlightenment is a possibility that both Buddhism and Christianity can help one another to understand and attain, for Buddhism has the wisdom to help one realize the wonder of the "I," and Christian faith brings knowledge of the personal, loving God. Through Christian enlightenment, then, one becomes not only awake but a person — one who *"belongs-to* God," and who can give and receive love. Christian enlightenment is what all people hunger for.

"Who are you, Gautama?"
"I am awake!"
"Who are you, Saint John the Evangelist?"

47

"I am the one loved by God!"
"Who are you, reader of these words?"

ESSENCE AND EXISTENCE

Reality is *both* one and many.

Intuition and feeling know the unitive aspect. Sensory information and reason focus on particularity.

The rational self knows God as Thou. The intuitive, feeling self knows God as the very light of the soul.

I think, I choose: essence.

Beyond thinking and choosing: existence.

Do choice and conceptualization cease with the experience of unity?

Life goes on, but without a willful agent. The "I" is there, but nonasserting. The "I" enjoys and continues to know that it must be a particularity, for it is not privy to the thoughts and feelings of others and cannot will for them. Those who say particularity is an illusion are themselves deluded.

When existence is realized, the illusion of particularity as ultimate truth is lost. Particularity in unity is realized. Now life will begin!

Look around you. Everything is creation-manifesting-God, if only you have eyes to see and a heart to feel.

Part II

Dynamics of Mystical Transformation

Intellectuals who write about mysticism are like men who write about pregnancy: They can say a lot of things that are true, but they do not know the Relationship, the Unity, the Experience. Better to be pregnant with God than to be a theological obstetrician.

ANTHROPOLOGY

1. Awareness is.
   It cannot be reduced
   to simpler components.

2. What *is* awareness?
   Who knows!
   Perhaps it is ...
   > the light of the soul.
   > God.
   > the True Self.

   Who knows!
   What awareness is cannot be defined.
   That awareness is cannot be denied.

3. For most, awareness is colored by desires.
   which are, in turn,
   generated by emotional states such as
   > insecurity,
   > shame,
   > resentment.

   Desires arise to compensate these pains.
   Ignorant thinking
   based on irrational beliefs
   about the self and reality
   keep one caught up in desire.
   Thus, for most, awareness is introverted

and caught up in preoccupation
over the fulfillment of desires.

4. When awareness is colored by pain,
   then the world and others are seen
   through a filter of desires:
   as being for or against
   the attainment of our desires.
   This is the origin of friends and enemies,
                   of good and bad,
                   of love and hate.

5. When awareness is colored
   by emotional pain and desires,
   the attender in consciousness is a small self,
   a self-concerned "I."
   This "I" experiences itself as real,
   owing to the felt reality
   of the emotions and desires
   that keep it preoccupied,
   the behaviors that proceed
   from its decisions,
   and the ripples these behaviors cause
   in the world.

6. When awareness is freed from desire,
   there is no small "I."
   Rather, the attender is synonymous
   with awareness itself,

and with all sensations,
thoughts, and feelings
that enter the field of awareness.
Such awareness is limited only
by the body's fixation in time and space.

7. In the state of pure, or cosmic, attention,
sensory perception is uncontaminated
by thoughts, feelings, and desires.
There is just-seeing, hearing,
smelling, and touching.
Feelings come and go,
but they do not disrupt sensory perception.

8. Will can be used to focus awareness,
to concentrate and intensify awareness
in a certain direction.
Volitional awareness is defined as
paying attention.

9. When the will is open
to relationship and engagement in life,
attention is also opened
to become cosmic and pure.
This openness of the will is called *agape*.
Agape is the only stance that maintains
the will in openness
and awareness in purity.

10. Lack of openness to relationship
    results in contraction of the will,
    and, hence, a constriction of attention.
    Therefore, openness
    to loving relationship with all
    is the only antidote
    to the misery of the small self.

11. Rational thinking directs the will.
    The will focuses awareness.
    Awareness presents data
    to the rational mind.
    These are the three
    irreducible and interrelated
    dynamics of consciousness.
    They are the spiritual qualities
    of human beings,
    incarnated in a body,
    conditioned and formed
    in a body in a culture,
    and freed from the limitations
    of the body at death.

12. The assault of evil
    is directed against reason.
    If people can be convinced
    that they need lots of irrelevant things,
    or that they can be okay

only if others approve them,
or that they must be perfect
and in control
to be safe,
then they will live in insecurity.
This contracts the will
and constricts attention.
This is the meaning of sin.

13. There is no liberation for the ignorant,
for those who can be persuaded
    to be fearful,
for those who do not value their worth,
for those who hold on to resentments.
Their rational intelligence is distorted.
Their attention is narrow and defensive.
Where there is ignorance,
there is superficiality
and lack of wholeness:
a fallen creature.

14. The struggle to know truth
is a struggle to free the will and awareness
from the ensnarements of evil.

15. Freedom from ignorance
does not lie in accumulating information,
but in knowing truth.

16. Truth is that toward which reason tends
    when one lives with
    > one's *own* questions,
    > honors these questions,
    > and struggles to answer them honestly.

17. In the struggle to answer one's questions,
    the mind is tamed,
    the will is directed toward its proper end,
    and awareness is progressively expanded.

18. The final Truth
    is nonconceptual mystery —
    just as the origin of awareness and will
    cannot be defined.
    The final Truth is ineffable;
    it cannot be contained.
    This does not mean
    that Truth is an illusion,
    or that the struggle to know Truth
    is a waste of time.
    It means only that Truth
    is not-knowing as well as knowing.
    It means that Truth is "seen" in awareness,
    and loved with the will,
    even as it is grasped by reason.

19. The three movements in the spiritual life
    are clear:

A. Recognition of one's condition
by practicing honesty

B. Resolution of one's emotional pain
through forgiveness

C. Retraining the mind
to meet one's true needs
by striving to understand truth
and practicing loving relationship
skills

20. In summary:
Awareness "sees" the activities
of the will and intellect,
and is, in turn,
freed by their loving direction.

ENLIGHTENMENT

1. In the lower, egoic states,
   awareness
   is identified with and reflected by
   self-concept.
   Intelligence and will, too,
   are bound up in self-concept.
   This is the small self,
   or mental ego.

2. The ego can be seen "from the outside"
   by a greater See-er,
   such as in a dream,
   where one sees and feels oneself.
   Who is this great See-er?
   Who is this unborn, serene
   Attender-of-my-life?
   It is the True Self.
   It is the sun seeing its sunbeam.

3. The True Self
   is the deepest subject of awareness.
   It is a direct experience
   of oneself as subject.
   This subjectivity
   is identical with awareness,
   and not inferior to it in any way.

4. The small self, or ego,
   is the object of awareness,
   a reflection of oneself, a self-image.
   The ego is awareness
   emotionally bonded to self-concept.
   It is reflexive consciousness.

5. In the True Self state,
   awareness, reason, and will are one.
   Awareness is intelligently loving.
   Intelligence is lovingly aware.
   Love is intelligently aware.
   Nonreflectively, nonconceptually so.

6. To live in the True Self state
   is to be-here-now-in-love,
   without distraction,
   without reflection,
   without reservation.
   This is ecstasy, for it is being-in-God.

7. Everyone experiences the True Self state
   in moments of ecstasy.
   The problem is that we believe
   external circumstances
   and material substances
   account for our ecstasies.
   Thus do we try to replicate the experience
   through these circumstances and things.

We need only drop the "I want,"
and there is ecstasy.

8. The "I" cannot be dropped
   as long as

>   ignorance,
>   shallowness,
>   emotional pain,
>   desires,
>   and addictions

   still persist.

9. As the mind is being healed and retrained,
   the True Self state emerges gradually,
   becoming more and more
   a *permanent state*
   as our growth and healing progress.

10. In the True Self state,
    happiness is unconditioned
    by any external contingencies.
    To maintain the True Self state,
    one need only stop disturbing oneself.
    Happiness exists when the mind
    stops creating unhappiness.

11. It is rare
    that one lives in the True Self state
    constantly each day.

Even the best of saints fall.
But these falls are the exception,
not the norm.
The saint gets up,
　　　　forgives,
　　　　and moves on.

12. When others see a True Self,
they see only an ordinary person.
Looking more attentively,
others will note the ease and serenity
that characterize the movements
of a True Self.
Through the True Self's actions,
the beauty of God's incarnate Word
is revealed.

13. In the True Self, we are simply human.
We are also
God-manifesting-as-the-person-we-are.
This is what it means to be human.

14. In the True Self,
the See-er sees all things.
In being seen, all things are changed.
What is Real
is validated, loved, and energized.
What is unreal falls away.

15. In the True Self,
    a person is a chakra,
    an energy organ through which God
            sees
            and loves
            and knows
    Himself/Herself in creation.
    The organ is real.
    It may distort or constrict the Light.
    But the organ is not the Light.
    It is illuminated.

16. All people — indeed, all creation —
    are Light-manifestors.
    If they are not manifesting Light,
    it is because intelligence and will
    are distorted.
    Even the innocent creation
    can be so distorted by people.
    How ridiculous,
    the behavior of a "trained watchdog."

17. The True Self "knows"
    without knowing how it knows
    what it knows.
    It can explain its insights
    in terms of concepts
    familiar to the intellect,

but it does not know
how it has arrived at these insights.
They come into the mind
like air into the nose.
It is as though the mind now participates
in a larger MIND,
as a brain cell
participates in the life of the mind.

CHRISTOLOGY

1. Christ is a vessel
    through which Light shines clearly.
    To look to him
    is to be drawn to Light.

2. Christ is Teacher and Model
    who focuses the will and intelligence
    in the Light.

3. Christ is Risen Guru.
    He is available to all who seek him.

4. Christ is Eucharist.
    We consume him,
    and so become part of him.
    He absorbs us into his Body
    by becoming part of our own.

5. Christ is Yogi.
    He yokes himself to his followers
    and moves them to undertake
    disciplines of transformation.

6. Christ is Heart-Master.
    Contact with him
    communicates the grace of his heart
    to the heart of the devotee.
    He gratuitously gives devotees

an experience of his own life,
imprinting his life in the mind.
By loving him, we become like him.

7. Christ is Son of the Father.
   He transforms his followers
   to see as he sees.
   His followers see with his own eyes,
   recognizing creation
   to be gift of the Father.

8. Christ is Redeemer.
   He accomplishes in us
   what we could never accomplish
   on our own,
   raising us from the pit of ego-bondage,
   to experience his own, magnificent Light.

9. Christ is the Ground of my neighbor's soul.
             Do I know this?
             Do I act accordingly?

10. Christ is Victor over evil.
    He strips it of its terror,
    revealing its destiny to be empty.

11. Christ is Risen.
    There is no permanent death.
    This life is a stage of growth.

12. Christ is Friend,
        ever-approachable,
        ever-interested,
        ever-present,
            to those who call upon him
                in faith.

13. Christ is God's blessing to this world,
        and reassurance
        that we have not been forgotten.

MYSTICAL THEOLOGY

1. Just as the body is already in the soul
     and the soul in the body,
   so, too, God is already in the soul,
     and the soul is in God.

2. God is always present to the soul,
          giving it life,
          loving it,
          attempting to lead it
   to become what God has created it to be.

3. Attachments and addictions
   create disturbances in the soul
   that prevent one from knowing
     God's presence
   and responding to the leadings
     of the Holy Spirit.

4. Nevertheless,
   even in this state of disturbance,
   one can begin to relate to God
   in whatever way is most meaningful.
   Jesus Christ is God's invitation
   to a return to full union.

5. When we love God and others
   while dropping attachments
   and addictions,

the false self will be put to death
and the True Self born.
This is a painful process —
a cross that heals the soul.

6. Through the dark nights
    of transformation,
   the soul is drawn
   into deeper and deeper realms of silence
   that transcend thought and feeling.
   Here, God's presence is known intuitively,
   and the soul becomes increasingly free
   to follow the leadings of the Spirit
   without being disturbed by
           attachments,
           addictions,
           and other worldly influences.

7. Thus it is that the soul is divinized,
   or made able to know God
   as Christ knows God.
   This is the fruit of the spiritual journey,
   and the reason for which we were created.

Part III

Exercises for Breaking Free

When the water in the pond is calm,
the dirt settles, and one can see the bottom.
When the mind is free from disordered desires,
the True Self can shine forth.

HOW TO DISTURB YOURSELF
MOST OF THE TIME
An Awareness Exercise

1. Think about all the possible negative things that might happen to you and your loved ones. Dwell on these negativities!

2. Tell yourself you're not okay now — that the circumstances of your life are not right for you to experience serenity and happiness, or that you'll be okay when...(but not now).

3. Spend lots of time thinking judgmental thoughts about yourself and other people. Dwell on your own and others' negative qualities.

4. Be a perfectionist. Have lots and lots of "shoulds" in your head regarding yourself and others. Then you can do all of the above most of the time.

5. Tell yourself you need other people's approval and admiration. Spend lots of time thinking about how to get this.

6. Try to control the behavior of other people. This one's guaranteed.

7. Watch competitive sports on TV. Strongly identify with one or another team, and get emotionally involved in the games.

8. Watch lots of TV and listen to the radio. Keep your environment filled with such noise. Avoid silence at all costs.

9. Nurture a grudge against another. Fantasize all kinds of ways to put the other in his or her place.

10. Stay in an unhealthy relationship. Be a victim! "It's God's will."

11. Eat junk food, drink alcohol and/or lots of coffee and high-sugar beverages.

12. Keep expanding your material wants. How dare the "Joneses" show you and your family up.

13. Cut down on your sleep. Stay up late at night watching TV or reading trashy novels.

14. Don't exercise! Be a couch potato.

15. Avoid contact with the outdoors and nature. Who needs fresh air!

16. Be very attached to your own good opinion of yourself. Take your idea of yourself very

seriously, and get defensive if other people don't properly adore you.

17. Believe that life has no meaning...that death has the last word.

18. Avoid prayer at all costs. Or, if you do pray, spend most of your time telling God what you want instead of listening to what God wants. Then, get angry at God when you don't get what you asked for, and use this anger to justify yourself against God.

ATTITUDE CHECK

1. What do you want from God?

2. What feelings are you in touch with?

3. What preoccupying thoughts have you been holding? What feelings are attached to them?

4. How's your breathing? Are you able to relax and center in the navel plexus?

5. Have you been shaking your legs? What are they telling you?

6. Are you seeking a fix in your prayer and meditation?

7. What has been the quality of your awareness?

8. Have you been focusing on loving, or on being loved?

INNER TRANSFORMATION AND HEALING
A Guided Meditation, or Journaling Exercise

1. Pay attention to the kinds of thoughts, feelings, and images going on in your consciousness.

2. Identify preoccupations that seem to convey the theme "I'll be okay when..." Label all of these as specifically as possible. E.g., "I'll be okay when I lose twenty pounds."

3. Restate the preoccupation in a negative sense.
E.g., "I'm not okay because I'm twenty pounds overweight."

4. How do you feel about this "not being okay because"...?
E.g., "Because I'm overweight, I feel embarrassed and ashamed."

76

5. What are specific circumstances when you have felt this way?

   E.g., "I feel ashamed and embarrassed about my weight when I go to family get-togethers or parties."

   Allow yourself to feel these feelings.

6. What do you need from God, from yourself, or from other people when you feel this way?

   E.g., "When I feel ashamed and 'fat,' I need to know that I am still loved and valued as a person."

7. Invite the Holy Spirit to speak to you and console you in your feelings of pain. Pray for the grace to be healed from these painful emotions.

   See Rm. 8:35–39. Jn. 14:27–31. Mt. 11: 28–30.

8. Allow yourself to feel loved even in your pain.

9. Self-affirmation: Speak from your conscious, rational self a nurturing phrase to your emotional experience.

   E.g., "I'm a lovable person."

"You [inner child] are loved by me, no matter what."

10. Positive imaging: See yourself in a circumstance usually difficult for you; feel yourself as a loving, lovable person in this circumstance. Repeat your affirmation if necessary.

The Nature of Attachments

Desire: attraction of the will toward any particular person, place, or thing.

— It is natural and inevitable for a created being with needs to have desires;

— Our deepest, most fundamental desires are to live, to understand, and to be happy; these desires can ultimately be fulfilled only in God.

Disordered Desires: inappropriate attraction of the will toward any particular person, place, or thing.

— The fulfillment of such a desire hurts oneself or others; the pursuit of such a desire violates moral values;

78

— the cultivation of such a desire undermines the experience of God as the fulfillment of our deepest desire.

A. To have what you do not want (but what you cannot be rid of without violating your moral values).

B. To want what you do not have (in such a manner as to undermine your experience of what you need most...i.e., union with God).

Attachments: disordered desires that have become more or less habitual preoccupations of the mind and will.

A. Examples: trying to gain the approval of others, winning, controlling other people and circumstances, accumulating money or sexual experience, getting high on something, perfect work, losing weight, etc.

B. Effects on consciousness:
— Intellect is preoccupied with ways to get what you want and avoid what you don't want; other people are seen as a help or a hindrance to obtaining attachment; you become judgmental.

— Will is focused on getting what I want . . . selfishness.

— Emotional climate is disturbed. I feel anxiety about not getting what I want, and angry toward threats to my fulfillment.

— Attention is focused on past and future. The NOW is missed.

— The experience of God is as One who can help me get what I want.

Addictions: attachments that have become compulsive preoccupations. The mind and will are no longer capable of completely resisting indulgence.

The Spiritual Significance of Attachments/Addictions: They are our primary obstacle to experiencing peace, happiness, union with God.

How to Know If You Have Attachments

1. Do you experience anxiety over situations beyond your control?

2. Is your mind "noisy," preoccupied over concerns that you derive little pleasure in considering?

3. Is it difficult for you to enjoy the NOW because disturbing memories from the past or anxious concerns about the future intrude?

— If you answer yes to any of these questions, you have an attachment of some kind.

HOW TO DROP AN ATTACHMENT/ADDICTION

Symptoms of Attachment:

1. Anxious preoccupation: restless thinking, judgmentalism

2. Lack of serenity

Quick Way:

1. Notice anxious preoccupation and its major themes. Verbalize these to God.

2. If no immediate action is required, say the Serenity Prayer, asking God to care for specific things not in your control and to give you the grace to trust in God's providence in your life.

3. Bring your attention into the NOW, and do what you're doing. The anxious preoccupation will fall away in short order if you do not indulge it behaviorally or mentally.

For Stubborn Attachments and Addictions:

1. Notice your preoccupation and its major themes. Write these down.
   "I feel anxious about . . . because [consequences] . . ."

2. Turn each theme into a question:

   "How can I be sure that...?"

   "What should I say to impress So-and-so?"

   "How can I be sure I will have enough money?"

3. See how much this question has influenced your thinking and behavior.

   Make a list of past decisions and behavior related to this question.

   Ask God for the grace to be free of this disordered desire.

4. See how this behavior has affected you and others. Make a list.

5. Resolve to make amends where your behavior in reference to this issue has hurt another. Ask God for forgiveness (This can take the form of the Sacrament of Reconciliation).

6. What real need (if any) is this question addressing?

7. What is the appropriate or prudent way to meet this need?

8. In your imagination, see yourself meeting this need in an appropriate manner. Ask

for divine guidance to see how to do this, and to desire this kind of responsible behavior.

9. If old preoccupations arise, see and acknowledge them nonjudgmentally, but do not indulge them. This is the true meaning of abstinence. Bring your attention into the NOW, and do what you're doing. If it is time to meet your real need in the manner you decided on in the previous point, go ahead and do so in awareness and gratitude.

When All Else Fails

After you've been doing the above for some time, it may become obvious that a compulsive attachment is so deeply rooted that you need additional help. Do not hesitate to ask for it. Help is available in the various Twelve Step groups and in addiction-treatment programs.

THE SERENITY PRAYER: A Meditation

God, grant me the serenity to accept the things I cannot change,

What are the chief causes of my anxieties? Do I have any control over these people, things, circumstances? Am I willing to let go of what I cannot control?

courage to change the things I can,

What do I control? What can I do about my situation? I can always control my attitude — the way I relate to people, places, things, circumstances. How do I need to change my attitude?

and the wisdom to know the difference.

Knowing what is my business, the other's business, and God's business is hard. If I cannot control or change something, I need to let it go. I ask God to help me do so in trust.

Living one day at a time, enjoying one moment at a time.

(Am I now/here? If not, am I no/where? I ask the grace to be attentive to the NOW in loving readiness.)

85

Accepting hardships as the pathway to peace. Taking, as he did, this sinful world as it is, not as I would have it.

(My cross is the burden that loving commitment has brought me. Do I accept my crosses? Do I see how rejecting them makes me and others miserable? Do I know that crosses lead to growth?)

Trusting that he will make all things right if I surrender to his will,

Do I trust Him to care for things if I let go of control? Have I yet learned that his plans for me are best? Do I believe that in his will is my happiness? I ask for a growth in faith.

that I may be reasonably happy in this life,

Happiness is a consequence of living-here-now-in-love. Am I unconditionally happy? Whom do I blame for my unhappiness? Do I see that it is the way I react to life that causes happiness and unhappiness? I ask the grace to take responsibility for my own happiness.

and supremely happy with him forever.

"The sufferings of this age are nothing compared to the glory of the age to come" [Rm.

8:18]. Do I cling to this life? Do I fear death? Does the prospect of heaven give me hope and joy? I ask for the grace to be hopeful.

Dynamics of the Heart

1. Where your treasure is, there is your heart, or center.

2. Where your center is, there are your thoughts and feelings. The "computer mind" connects with the center via an "ultimate question," and is constantly working on this question.

3. As your thoughts and feelings go, so goes your behavior.

4. Behavior is a product of thought, feeling, centeredness, and reinforces patterns of thought and feeling in a center.

Changing Your Heart

5. What is your treasure?

    A. What does your behavior tell you?

    B. What do you feel excited about/drawn toward?

   C. What is the question to which your deepest thoughts are responding? Identify this question.

   D. What are the values implied in this deepest question?

   E. Where does this question come from? E.g., world, parents, Holy Spirit?

6. What have been the consequences to your life and others' in the living out of this question?

7. Do you wish to continue living out this question?

8. How does this question relate to Christ's questions of you?

   A. Will you let me love you?

   B. Will you love me with your whole heart, soul, mind, and strength?

   C. Will you seek first my Kingdom?

   D. Will you help me build my Kingdom on earth as in heaven?

9. Are you willing to continue placing these questions first, and resist the questions/ temptations of the world?

Living in the Center

1. To see and resist all that takes you away from Christ. Call it by name/identify the question it asks. Refuse the behavior.

2. To resolve emotional consequences of un-centered living through forgiveness, making amends.

3. To nourish mind and heart with good reading, teaching, music.

4. To grow in the center through prayer, meditation, sacraments.

Following Your Heart: General Principles

5. "Seek ye first the Kingdom of God and its righteousness, and all else will be given unto you" (Mt. 6:33).

6. Principle of synchronicity. You are drawn through your center to people, circumstances, books, etc., that deepen your life in that center. This can work for good or evil.

7. When in doubt, place your growth first, and you will usually end up serving the Kingdom as a consequence.

8. Never make an important decision when divided within yourself.

9. There is evil; there are forces of darkness that would like to steer you off your path. Stay awake!

10. If something is not true, then it is not about Love.

11. Live one day at a time, here/now/in-love. The question for each day: "What would you have me do and learn today, Lord?"

12. Examen: "What have I done and learned with you today, Lord?" "How did I stray from our union, Lord?" Note thoughts and feelings that arise in response to these questions. What false questions/issues did you get caught up in? Give praise and thanksgiving for times of union; ask pardon for separations.

GUIDELINES FOR CHRISTIAN PRAYER

The most important of all disciplines is prayer. By prayer, I mean opening our human consciousness to loving relationship with God. This can be done all through the day in simple acts of faith and love, but it is doubtful that we will do this well without the formal discipline of private prayer. It is good to spend time alone with God just as it is good to spend time alone with a lover. For beginners I recommend at least twenty minutes twice a day. As the spirit matures, one will want to spend longer periods.

There are two general types of Christian prayer: active and contemplative. In active prayer, we use our minds to relate ourselves to God by reading Scripture, pondering its meaning, and addressing our petitions to God. In contemplative prayer, we simply rest in the awareness of God's love for us. Typically, one begins the life of prayer using active methods, and these gradually give way to contemplation. As one grows in contemplative prayer, the human spirit becomes transformed by the Holy Spirit so that one habitually thinks, desires, and acts in accordance with God's plan. Contemplative prayer also awakens us to the experience I have called the True Self.

The method of prayer described below is an amplified version of centering prayer. This is a form of prayer that is still active, but it is highly receptive to the grace of contemplation. If you become too overwhelmed by distractions when attempting this kind of prayer, then this may indicate that you are not yet ready for it — that you would do better to quiet yourself, then to read and reflect on Scripture. Active prayer is by no means "second-rate." If you persist in active prayer, the mind will eventually become more silent, and this present form of prayer may come easier for you.

Amplified Method of Centering Prayer

1. Allow at least twenty minutes (perhaps after a period of reading and reflecting on Scripture).

2. Find a quiet place where you will not be disturbed by external circumstances.

3. Assume proper posture: back straight, chin parallel to the floor, right hand resting on the left hand. If you can sit on the floor, that is best; if not, a straight-backed chair or a prayer stool will do.

4. Offer your prayer time to God. Ask the Holy Spirit and your guardian angel to lead you in this prayer.

5. Close your eyes, or gaze gently at a place on the floor about three feet in front of you.

6. Become aware of the sensations in your body. Gently scan your body from toes to crown. As you notice your body, imagine that the Light of God is coming into your body through your awareness.

7. Become aware of your breathing. Breathe normally at first, then increase the depth of your breathing, not forcing anything. Inhale into your heart, then draw the breath into the navel area; exhale deeply from the navel area. Imagine that your inhalation is charged with the love of God, and your exhalation is discharging stress and negativity.

8. Simply rest in God's presence, using a simple word or phrase to maintain your openness to God. If you feel moved to complete loving silence, let go of the word or words. (Instead of using a word, you might also imagine that you are bathing in God's Light, and you might "feel" your spirit receiving this Light. You might also simply

open to God as a Presence in whom you live and move and have your being.)

9. When you become aware of thoughts that lead you away from this simple resting, return to the previous point. (If you have the gift of glossolalia and it suggests itself during this time of prayer, do give consent to it.)

10. Gently end the prayer experience when you are ready by opening your eyes. It is also good to stand up and walk slowly, right hand resting in the left, noting the feel of your body moving — especially the sensations under your feet. Five minutes of this "walking meditation" are usually sufficient to make the transition from prayer into everyday living. Many find it necessary to wait another fifteen minutes or so before reading or engaging in focused mental concentration. Do not judge the experience according to how you feel right after prayer. The effects are sometimes more obvious hours later.

AFFIRMATIONS FOR REALIZING
THE TRUE SELF

(Repeat slowly, mindfully, attempting to experientially comprehend the truth in each statement.)

"You are as You are, O Lord, and I am as I am."
(*Cloud of Unknowing*)

"I am the one who is here, now, alive in this moment."

"I am the one who is reading these words, seeing out of these eyes."

"I am the one who is loved by God in this very moment."

"I am because You have made me, O Lord."

"I am here, now, freely willing to love."

"I am not my thoughts; I am not my feelings; I am not my desires; I am not what others think I am — I am the one who *has* thoughts, feelings, desires. I am the one whom others see."

"I am, and others are, too. I am me; they are themselves."

"I am, and it is very good to be. Thank You, Lord."

CHARACTERISTICS OF DETACHMENT

1. To allow no one, no thing, and no circumstance to determine whether you will be happy or not

    (NOTE: To be emotionally affected is normal, but do not be emotionally determined by these factors)

2. To prefer God's will over anything else, believing that in God's will is your real happiness to be found

3. To choose to do God's will as you understand it, regardless of what other people think about you for doing so

4. To fully accept yourself and all your natural desires

5. To pursue your natural desires without attachment and in consideration of moral values

Part IV

Nuggets from the Stream of Life: Proverbs and Practical Wisdom for Spiritual Living

A nugget is a piece of gold "in the raw." It must be melted down and purified to yield its treasure. The same may be said of spiritual nuggets like those that follow. They are presented "in the raw," each of them needing the fires of your own life to draw out their truths.

Don't rush through these proverbs. Let each speak to your experience to validate and challenge your living. Then will the gold be found deep in your own heart.

To deny your neediness is to deny your creatureliness. True enlightenment is not the absence of needs but the recognition that our greatest need — union with God — is fulfilled in each breath and moment.

You can do something only, always, in the NOW. What you cannot do NOW, leave alone. Drop it! Simply drop it! Come back to NOW. It's all there is.

It really doesn't matter *what* you are doing (so long as it is not sin). It is *how* you do something that matters. In every moment, there is God. To do what you are doing in union with God: This is happiness.

Accept whatever state of consciousness you are experiencing now in gratitude. Do not say, "I should be experiencing my life another way!" This is self-rejection, the cause of division.

Right practice — loving now — is far more important than anything else. This practice is happiness itself. It leads to understanding, and not vice versa.

When you interact with others in a manner unto growth and fun, God moves among and through you, enriching the human bond. When you refuse to interact with others in this manner, you become a "knot," blocking the flow of God in the human community.

"Lost in my thoughts!" So true: That is where most people are.

Anything that intensifies separateness and narrow identification is to be avoided. For example, winning, competitive sports, having, getting, most philosophy and theology, most television programs. Only total passivity to the Life Force within will do. That which obstructs its flow is to be avoided.

When thinking accomplishes nothing, drop it by switching the attention to breathing. Breathe naturally, normally, each breath received in gratitude for the gift of life, and for the "Breather" in the soul.

The intellect is servant, not master. It provides vision, which is necessary. But it cannot be the center in which attention rests, for then it becomes puffed with pride and turns the self and the world into a conceptual system, which it defends and presides over. This is vanity and great illusion!

Without love, the Light of consciousness fades, so that consciousness is just a computer spinning out programs to solve problems it has created for itself.

You have no shame, but you still have pride! Surprised? Remember this: Pride came before shame in Eden.

The namer has become the named, the hunter caught in his own snare: the False Self.

Can't find yourself? Just open your eyes! There you are: looking.

If you're out of touch with your thoughts and feelings and experience a kind of tension and resistance to acknowledging limitations, there's probably a "should" somewhere blocking your awareness, attempting to force you into a role while filtering out all that does not fit this role. Drop it! Adults don't need shoulds anymore. Roles defined by shoulds kill the spirit. Only in authenticity and freedom can happiness be found.

When we are preoccupied, living is a fog of desires, unresolved emotional pain, intellectual confusion, a state of being asleep to ourselves and life: This is how most people live! How sad! How to wake them up?

A little actor on the stage: the false self (including, here, even the Christian Mental Ego).

Paradigmatic "stages of growth" are useful for validating broad, general patterns of human unfolding. They are maps of sorts, but not as precise as geographical maps. Learn the maps, then put them down and enjoy the scenery. Who would want to look at a map of the Alps when riding through them?

The surest sign of spiritual health is to be found in your ability to take an interest in other people, to really listen to them, and to be willing to help them in whatever manner is appropriate. When your spirituality does not produce this fruit, you are probably involved in delusions of some kind.

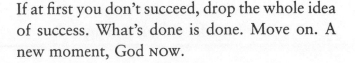

Do not repress memory, but do not cling to it, either. You are at least everything you have experienced. Your past is the record of your song and dance.

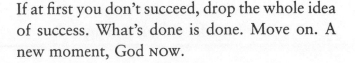

If at first you don't succeed, drop the whole idea of success. What's done is done. Move on. A new moment, God NOW.

No roles can maintain the True Self, although it can take on any role and play it in full awareness. The True Self "has" the role, not vice versa.

Creation is that through which God flows. God is the One who flows through creation. Creation needs God. God needs nothing, although without creation, God would have nothing to flow through.

Don't worry about anything — ever! What's done is done, and what will be will have to wait until NOW. Make amends if your past haunts you, and make plans if you must. But do it NOW.

If you desire true happiness, then spirituality will bring you there. If you seek more — wealth, power, recognition, being "special" — then spirituality will not be enough. Neither will anything else!

If you stand before God, another, and/or creation wanting to "get" something, you will be anxious and unfree. If you stand willing to love, accepting in gratitude what is given, you will be peaceful and free.

The purpose of thought/speech is to communicate about needs and perceptions. Multiply needs into wants and distort perception and thought increases: the noisy, disturbed mind.

The one who looks, the looking, and the seeing are one: how beautiful! "When the eye is single, the whole body will be sound!" How true!

Preoccupied? Lots of involuntary thoughts racing around? The data banks are searching. Searching for what? See if there is an issue to which you need to respond. If there is, then make a plan to do something about it and do it when appropriate. If there is no real issue, drop the useless thinking by shifting attention to the now, the senses, creation. Let the thought waves die out gently.

Sin is very pervasive. Its roots run very, very deep!

People are not really all that screwed-up! Let them rid themselves of a bit of pain through reconciliation, and loosen the hold on self-image and . . . there they are: just people.

Love is the only answer to all of your "problems." Even when you are in deep mental anguish — the worst of all pains — love is the only answer. In loving, the Spirit configures your energies unto wholeness and serenity — eventually, that is, and not without suffering.

In the end, attention/energy assumes the form, or thought, of you spoken by God. To let yourself go into the form that God has created you to be is contemplation.

True understanding is impossible to attain conceptually. To attempt this is like trying to define the smell of a rose or the experience of falling in love. The heart knows love and truth far more clearly than the intellect.

When you read, do so with an open mind, and in a spirit of detachment. Receive the words deep in your heart, but do not hold on to them. Notice your questions, welcome them, hold on to them, and let them bring forth their truth in due time.

Can there be attention without intention? Can there be intention without attachment? No to the first, yes to the second.

The false-self system is a mental-conceptual organization of life experiences and memories focused around a general emotional theme or motive — e.g., security, power, pleasure, recognition, etc.

The knowledge of God comes from a change in the knower produced by God. This is the grace of faith, without which one cannot know God.

Do not surrender your right to decide things for yourself to anyone — not even to Christ. Your life is your own, and Christ would have you live it and discover your way in honesty, questioning, and self-chosen surrender. He will teach and support.

Never abandon your common sense or your sense of humor. They will, without fail, keep you from going crazy.

Attention is a light that energizes. What you attend to, you energize. Beware! If you attend too long to temptation, it shall come to pass. If you keep your mind fixed on being-here/now/in-love-to-love, you will always be happy.

Nature is innocent and free. To be in touch with nature is to grow in freedom and innocence. Nature is not conscious, however, and it is totally without compassion. These are potentialities you must choose to develop to become truly human. Nature will not instill them into you.

Preoccupation is useless thinking. Useless thinking is thinking about that which does not concern you, that which you cannot change, and that which is not yours to do now. Withdraw your attention from all such useless thinking, and you will immediately feel better.

Say it: "I have choices!" Feel yourself alive as an individual human being. You *can* do what you want, but you do pay consequences for your choices. What are your consequences telling you?

Mind-intent is more important than states of mind. Let states of mind come and go, but hold fast to your willingness to love all things.

The kind of spiritual practice you undertake determines the kind of person you will become. This practice, in turn, is informed by your vision of life. Do not scorn good teaching! It has its place.

Habits of thought, speech, and attention concentrate energy in different parts of the body. These are uncoiled and healed as the Spirit cleanses the soul. Let it happen. Enjoy it.

The drop that falls into the ocean becomes one with the ocean: It becomes diffused — still itself; now, too, the ocean. It is simply no longer itself-as-drop, but is now itself-in-ocean. This is the meaning of death.

Love is not something we "should try to do" over and against other impulses. Love is who we are and what we do when we are not concerned about getting something for ourselves. To live and act in this way is the meaning of spirituality.

Just look and see from the heart. No thoughts. No judgments. Enlightenment! Indescribable bliss!

There can be no love without choice. How would you like it if someone said he loved you because he had do, because he feared the pains of hell? Spare me such a friend, O Lord! "Spare Me such a friend, O human!"

To know the better way and to refuse to follow it: This is a choice for sin and a building up of the false self.

There is nowhere to go and nothing to do to realize Eternal Life. Drop the false and live in the true and there it is, where it always has been. So...what does one do after this is seen? Enjoy! Meet your needs. Help others meet theirs. That is all!

Most heresy is very close to the truth — maybe only half a degree off. But this small distortion on a thousand-mile journey leads one far off course. Therefore, do not spurn dogma. It helps you keep your bearings.

When you talk, read, or write too much, the intellect and speech center can be overstimulated, and mental silence will be lost. This is understandable. How do you think your right arm would feel if you swung it round and round all day?

Every second all is new
when preconceptions are no more.

Words determine emotional reality. "I don't like living with kids!" produces a much different emotional reaction from "I'm tired right now, and feel bothered by my kids' noises." The second phrase is more honest and produces a less hostile reaction.

If one thing still seems better than another, one moment more full of life than another, one moment better than another — you are still immature. God saturates all moments and all things. To experience this is the end of desiring and preferring. Serenity!

A triangle is a form that may be expressed in an infinite number of ways. So, too, with Christ. He is the human form, and each person is a specific manifestation of what it means to be Christ.

Suffering is the gap that exists between what is and how you want things to be (or not be). Close the gap — no suffering!

You can experience the other as other only if you want nothing from the other but to give what is needed. When there is desire, the other is seen as for or against its fulfillment — not as a person.

If you are going to be alive anyway, you might as well strive to be as happy, peaceful, and free of turmoil as possible.

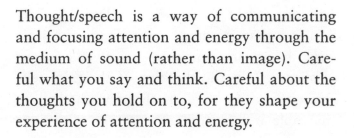

Thought/speech is a way of communicating and focusing attention and energy through the medium of sound (rather than image). Careful what you say and think. Careful about the thoughts you hold on to, for they shape your experience of attention and energy.

Paradigmatic conceptualization constricts attention and distorts energy along the lines suggested by the paradigm. This may represent an improvement over emotional consciousness, but it is an obstacle to spiritual enlightenment.

The great enemy lies in the good you are leaving behind. You know this, and you want to go back. Move on! The best is yet to come.

Thinking is not the enemy of silence. Useless thinking that conduces toward anxiety, jealousy, shame, or resentment — this is the enemy of silence. It is the thinking of the false self. Drop it, and the thinking that remains will be enjoyable and useful.

Do not "put on" or imitate anyone — not even the Lord Jesus Christ (apologies to Saint Paul). Instead, be-here/now/in-love, with your whole being awake, relaxed, intellect alert, memory available if needed, the heart ready to love. Do this as *you,* not someone else.

No need to "guard" your experiences of God and true life. That which guards and tries to perpetrate it is the obstacle to its ongoing realization.

Let the "chooser" step forward, out of the chatter and rumination, and let the choice be for here/now/loving-willingness — God! Then all shall be well.

Faith comes not from intellectual conviction, but from an open, trusting yes to God's invitation to loving unity. Of course, without intellectual conviction, the mind will not instruct the will to say yes. Even so, faith opens one to realms that the mind cannot know.

What do you want? It is important to know, for there is always the danger that your wish will come to pass. Would you really be happy if your wants were fulfilled?

The emptiness of the true mystic is not merely psychological vacuity (which is quietism), but the negation of self-will for the sake of loving union.

The key to now-living is: "Do what you are doing." This means letting go of what you are not doing, or cannot be doing. It is in reflecting, comparing, and judging that the false self is born, and these operations are starved out when you simply "do what you are doing," and only that. Then, too, psychic energy is transformed, spiritualized, and attention becomes clear and peaceful.

If you want anything more than to be-here/now/in-love-to-love, you will not be happy, but in a state of disordered desiring.

Don't know how to love God? Very well, love people and creations, and that will be enough.

Realize the divine within? You cannot even realize the consciousness of your spouse, whom you see and touch and know so well. Experience the consciousness of another — yes! But this is not the same as realizing another's consciousness.

There is no right way to pray. Technique is incidental. Whatever helps you to surrender totally to God — body, mind, and spirit — is the right technique.

The True Self is the one who is here through all the changes in life. To identify with any of life's changing circumstances and experiences is to lose the True Self to a "my" self. The True Self is not "mine." It is just-me.

We receive him and become one with him who is one with the Father in the Spirit. He takes the whole soul into this union. Eucharist!

Drop your attachments and follow your heart. Drop dissipating thoughts and behaviors, and the healthy "you" will emerge most naturally and beautifully. Quit making yourself sick, and you shall be well. How simple it is! How difficult!

You are not alone in caring for your growth. You are responsible, but there is much help available: Christ, the angels, saints, and the Church on earth are here to help you. They want to help you. Let them.

If union with God is the ideal, then it must be admitted that this union must take place here/now, for that is where God is, and it must be in-love, for that is how God is.

In the end, there are only two considerations that matter: agape, and non-agape. Are you here/now, open, willing to give of yourself, open to receiving and enjoying others and creation? If not, you are in non-agape, constricting attention, desiring, cultivating self-states of consciousness — anxiety!

Part of your mind is a talking computer. You are not this. You can talk to this part of yourself and reprogram the computer.

What is happening, subject-to-subject, is the greatest mystery. I and Thou become We, which is more than I plus Thou. This can be experienced and to some extent described, but never defined.

They are, every one of them, your brothers and sisters, made of exactly the same "stuff" that you are. They are, most of them, caught up in desire, delusion, and ignorance, just like you once were. Love them for who they are, not for who they "think" they are.

Life is not a torment to be endured, but a journey to be lived one day at a time. Let each day be new. No projecting onto tomorrow.

Comparing, judging, defending: this is the cancerous energy of the false self manifesting in the mind. See this, but do not judge yourself. To do so would only spread the cancer. See it, but don't indulge it. If you don't use it, you lose it.

Christ himself speaks through the intuitive function. His Word elicits an immediate consensual response from the other faculties. When Christ speaks — even of doing a hard thing — his words bring peace. Other "voices" leave the mind disturbed.

The leaders of the world religions sit on a treasure of gold (their mystical traditions), tossing out Mardi Gras tokens to the people.